The 2nd Time I Fell In Love With Jesus

A Testimony of a Pastor's Daughter

Nodia Samuels

AuthorHouse™
1663 Liberty Drive
Bloomington, IN 47403
www.authorhouse.com
Phone: 1 (800) 839-8640

Published by AuthorHouse 02/07/2019

ISBN: 978-1-5462-7896-2 (sc)
ISBN: 978-1-5462-7898-6 (hc)
ISBN: 978-1-5462-7897-9 (e)

Library of Congress Control Number: 2019901308

DEDICATION

Dear mom,

THANK YOU.

It's funny because I say it all the time but this time it's different. As I sit in the office at work I'm reminded of one of the many moments where you said that you would fight me, for me. I've spent my entire life fighting for everything except myself. I fought for independence, love, freedom, affection, friends, family and men. All were delicate flowers planted in my bosom only to be smothered and wither away. You taught me the painful art of letting go. The day you let me go I felt as though God didn't exist. I plunged into a life that only existed behind closed curtains and under stained bedsheets, my soul was now only collateral damage and the remnant of a war that I had been fighting with myself. It was around that time I ran into Jesus. At the first glance he intrigued me, but my pain had overshadowed my hope of ever loving again. Day by day as his assurance gave me security and my weakness perfected his strength I began to trust him. Mom I'm sorry, because the day you let me go you lost your best friend. God had a divine plan. You found love. I found God. All those years I spent buried in the dirt made me forget who I was, but as I emerged I came up with a new form. As I have matured I now expose my scars and wounds allowing the secretly broken to take first class seats on my journey of healing. I came to my senses and you embellished my hands with your finest rings and have clothed me in graciousness. You stripped your strength and showed me your nakedness and I will always choose to cover you because of it. Mom you are made of righteousness and selflessness.

You sit comfortably in uncomfortable situations with grace and class as if it were the Shekinah Glory. I love you. I looked back into yesterday and I saw you in a boxing ring fighting against 17-year-old me. Mom you won! I stare into the mirror and there are fragments of your strength connected to my limbs. I see your morals on my chest, your strength in my feet, your resilience in my spine. Mom, you did it. You've refined me into a glass of grace. I'm not finished though, I am still becoming, and only because you have exemplified true womanhood. I love that your signature is penned beside all of my successes. I celebrate and honor you. I love you. I just want a quarter of you and with that ONLY I know I can CONQUER Anything.

PRELUDE

The Man at The Bus Stop...

Her: God, Help...

Him: Hey, Wassup!

Her: *Crooked Look* Can I help you?

Him: You look like you need some help?

Her: I'm good, Thanks.

Him: Can I borrow a dollar?

Her: Borrow or Have? cause you don't look like you can pay me back.

Him: If you knew who I was you would give me $20.

Her: And if you knew who I was you'd give me $20 too *Laughs*

Him: Can I have your heart?

Her: Love don't live here anymore.

Him: ...But it has before, and it was broken by deception and abuse.

Her: How do you know me?

Him: No, the question is, how do you not know me?

Most people don't believe me when I talk about God. To them it seems unrealistic, to have someone who can love you into a better being, someone who is perfected in my weakest moments, someone who's joy causes peace and who's peace passes understanding. Sounds like a fairytale, right? I think the best part about my God is knowing that he's real for myself. Experiencing him for myself and on my level. KNOWING THAT SO MUCH that I don't need a trip to Israel, a compelling story or even to witness a miracle to believe. Because I experience his realness every minute of every day. So, no, I don't need the politics and semantics to confirm who I already know he is. All I need is him. And most times when I'm feeling lonely it feels good to know that even though everyone can have him, he's still ALL MINE.

I met Jesus at 12 years old and I loved him, but I fell **IN** love with him long after that. At 12 I had felt the quickening of the Holy Spirit during a short praise session at my church. Teacher Rhonda had led that day and as she sang an old sankee (A short chorus) that I had not yet understood I felt a presence lift me off my seat and took hold of me in that very moment, and nothing was the same.

When my body laid down in the grave
Then my soul cry out for Joy!
Rock Oh my Soul Rock Oh my Soul!

Looking back now I recognize that everything I knew to be true shifted at that moment. Church was no longer boring. God felt like someone I didn't mind getting to know. There is this misconception that Pastor's kids automatically are born with Holy Ghost fire, that's not true and I'm here to dispel the myths. The sankee foretold the story of my life in advance. Not too long after this, life would take me on a journey that kills me, and I would reborn in a garment of praise because I made use of my redemption.

This book is not a memoir, it is not a story, it's not even a self-help. It is a testimony of my life, of my journey, of my struggle, of my trial, my temptation and my victory; along with some information I think everyone should know but doesn't have access to. I want you to know you're not alone, so I am baring some of my wounds hoping that someone will be encouraged. I told someone about my book and when they ask me what it was about and what type of book it was I wasn't sure what to say it's not that I didn't know what I was writing but it was because everything I wrote was under the divine inspiration of god. This book is not about me. it's about you. Everything that I say, every moment of transparency, and every confession. I have filleted my heart on the table for you. So that you can see that there is life after death, that there is hope after dismay, and that there is love after the lost. So please don't read with the intention to understand me. Read hoping that somewhere between the pages you will find you. Without having known you I believe that you are powerful. I want the world for you because that is what I want for me. So, before we go any further I would like to pronounce a blessing on you my love. May you be blessed from the crown of your head to the bottom of your feet. May you laugh with your entire being and love with all your might. May you find the missing piece that life's puzzle has camouflaged. May generational curses crumble at the sight of you. May everywhere that you place your hands turn to pure gold and May everlasting peace dwell in you infinitely.

Thank you so much in advance for your time and your patience in reading my baby, my book, my testimony.

Momma and Me

SLAP! All I could've felt across my face was this pulsating numbness when my mother had slapped me for what felt like the first time. I had been asking her for something that I can't even remember and when I was told no, I responded "You're not even my mom!" I think that may have been the moment she realized this parenting thing is no joke. Mom packed up my stuff and shipped me off to Grandma's where everything was different.

Grandma was my biological mother. HERE'S THE STORY, my mom took me from my grandmother when I was three months and I've been hers ever since, well until THAT day. It is not the regular Older sister raised younger one story because she is my mother. Ever since my mom took me she has handled every aspect of my life. Even when I lived at grandma's she still took me school shopping and gave me allowances, was over like almost every day, but I guess God was taking her through her own process. See my mom has no birth children, but that's her story to tell not mine. All I know is that God sent me for her and prepared her for me. I know there is no such thing as a perfect mother, but Mrs. Esther Primus comes fairly close. Anyways back to Granny…

Grandma's house was a circus compared to mines, she's a good doer so there were always random children everywhere and extended family staying over until they found a place. Crackheads across the street, Chinese store and corner store down the block and a McDonalds on the other end. Grandma lived in Bushwick. That's in Brooklyn. At grandma's house I only got one dollar because there were about five other kids who had to get too, I always had to wait for the bathroom and worst of all I had to eat whatever they cooked which by the way was things I don't eat, grandma's house SUCKED! Mom came over all the time and I went weekends, but I still had to live at Grandma's.

I've always felt like living with my grandmother messed up our relationship. While Getting to know her and being raised by her even for that short amount of time we bumped heads a lot and I think it's because of her troubled past. See grandma was abused in all sorts of ways and the way she was raised can be described as heart wrenching, she doesn't talk about it with us but when our aunts and uncles are over they all discuss the ghost of their pasts. I wonder how different things would be if maybe she wasn't abused or beaten or even left to live with extended family who sowed seeds of anger and distrust into her life. Living with my grandmother while I was younger was complicated. I lived by the rules of my mom, but I was able to break them when grandma wasn't looking. My grandma's childhood reflected heavily in the way she raised me. Simple things that would be described as authoritarian parenting today would be hard evidence of her childhood. I remember one time getting a spanking for something I didn't do because she didn't give me time to explain. Later on that evening someone told her of my innocence and she started crying and yelling at me asking me why I didn't speak up and say anything. As much as she yelled and cried I didn't feel anything because even as a child I noticed she wasn't talking to me, she was talking to herself. So clearly, I could see her projecting her feelings on to me. *At* first, I was upset throughout childhood but as I got older I just became empathetic, because I realized she was raising me the only way she knew how. Many times after I could sense her remorse for her harsh correction. Even still I found forgiveness a hard gift to give. I share this with you not to make you hold negative thoughts towards her or your own parent, but to help you understand how deep the issues in your relationship with your parents/Care-Givers might run. A lot of times we hold hostility towards our family for things that they've done but take no time to listen to their stories. It will not excuse the behavior, but it can definitely enlighten and give you new perspective on the person that you are judging. Trace your family's patterns and find the history behind who they are. It will help you to deal with them. My relationship with my grandmother is in better place because of it. I remember hearing a member of my church testify about being molested and after the service she said to the woman "You know that happened to me too, but that's how it is back home (home is Trinidad). I remember thinking "wow so that's why she acts like that". It was then I knew I couldn't change her, and I didn't want to anymore, so I changed myself. I am happy to say that the love of God has profoundly been a testament in her life and she embodies Paul's words in the bible that says we must die daily. She is the one person I thought would never change but continues to do so every day and I know it's not her, it's the love of Christ that lives in her heart. I thank God for the day I stopped trying to change others and focused on changing myself. It caused me to rely on the only person capable of truly changing someone, Jesus. One day there was a fire and as I stood in the front yard with my pajamas watching the flames burn, of course mom pulled up like superwoman as always and took me back. It was clear, to us at least, that She was my mom and I was her daughter.

It was our destiny. Some people just can't let it go through! You should see the fire we breathe when out of order people say, "that's not your real mother" and that's why we decided not to tell anyone our truth, but just like rivers, mouths run. By the time I was 13 news had spread that Esther is not my mother. I cried the day I overheard it, it's not like I hadn't already known but I had chosen that it doesn't matter, why couldn't everyone else let it go? My mom was my choice, I wanted her even though I knew she was tough, even though I knew I would never have the privileges of the other kids, it didn't matter she was mines and I was hers. I had a father, but I never really knew him. My biological dad's name was Hector Samuels. He and my biological mom(grandma) met here in the united states fell in love and had me. I have no idea how the story went afterwards but they broke up and when I was old enough to know I had a dad he was living in Guyana. So, we had no relationship. Of courseeeee my grandmother would disagree trying to prove a Father-Daughter connection with about 4 summer vacations in Guyana where he lived and some jewelry on birthdays. I didn't know the man! He never called and when he did it would be this awkward conversation avoiding the fact that he lives in another country with another family and doesn't know anything about me. I always told myself maybe it was better not to know him, maybe he was this evil person that I should be thankful for not knowing, it helped me cope. When he died I was 12 years old. My mom laid me on her chest and she gently stroked my hair, I remember thinking that she might be sad and need some cheering up but about 10 minutes into it she said to me "Baby girl, your dad died", to this day I haven't responded. I cried a little bit and the next day was like any other. Turns out, When I had finally came to terms with my father's death which was a couple days after, his girlfriend had already had the funeral. I handled it pretty well, I've always handled death well (except for one). I think my mom had noticed my tough exterior from a young age and gave me an extra supply of love because of it. Her love however was only almost as strong as her protection.

My mom is the definition of overprotective and should be the poster child for helicopter parenting. I mean this lady would spy on me while I walked home from school, check my book bag, forbid me from sleepovers and never let me out of her sight. So, I bet you know what came out of that, an extra sneaky little church girl! My natural rebellious nature made me tell so many lies that I had to memorize them. Our relationship was strong, but boy did I hide things. I spent my entire 7th grade year switching out of my uniform into regular clothes for school. We had this tacky dress code of khaki pants and a yellow shirt that I absolutely hated not to mention it did nothing for my figure, I mean how would the boys notice me? Mom always told me that you can attract men without serving up your body on a silver platter, but I never took anything she said seriously. That statement applied to men and I was dealing with boys so Bump that, I'm wearing my miniskirts and crop tops. It totally worked I mean I got so much attention, I didn't like it all the time, but I rathered the unwanted attention than none at all. Things were great, I had lots of friends, already had my first boyfriend, and was with boyfriend number two! Everything was going just as I planned until Parent-Teacher's Conference. Mommy NEVER misses it. Which is why I have no idea why I thought it smart to be BAD GYAL 2.0 in school. As my teacher pulled out my report card the number 55 multiplied itself by 6 and equaled that I had failed every class, except art. As we walked to the art room I could feel my life span shortening and my final hour approaching. The art teacher was this short Spanish lady with hair straight out of a grease movie, and zero English skills. Already knowing what was coming I told my mom we should skip the art teacher since I had done so well and got a 90 in the class. Like any Caribbean mother she replied that she will be talking to EVERY last one of my teachers. As we walked into the art room the teacher began to greet us but the sight of me apparently was her worst nightmare, she began shouting in a mixture of Spanish and English. Mommy didn't speak Spanish, but one thing was understood, and it was that the 90 on my report card was a mistake. It was confirmed when my short grease like Spanish teacher referred to me as Brittany. The teacher had given me a good grade because she didn't know my name, she thought it was Brittany. At that moment I felt as mother earth should crack open and suck me into her core until Parent teacher's night was over. We went from class to class and teacher to teacher hearing about my potential, horrible behavior, missing homework assignments, recurrent absences and my lack of motivation. Most parents would be shouting over the rooftops but not my momma she was always so classy. She smiled, shook hands, made jokes and even went on to have long discussions about the public education system. With all the calmness in the atmosphere my teacher still however noticed that My demeanor was despondent. He thought it was because I was disappointed in myself, NOT EVEN. That semester was one of the best in Junior high. He didn't understand that my mother was a woman of God, A MIGHTY woman of God who teaches the gospel, bind up broken hearts and set captives free, ALLAT. It meant she knew scripture and you know what scripture says?

"Spare the rod, Spoil the child". That scripture is what replayed in my head as my mother literally ran to the car and pushed 80 mph in 30mph zone all the way to the house. We got home and the same spirit that brought that scripture to my remembrance told me to walk straight to my room. As she followed me I prepared myself for her true response to that night, the door locked, and the rod was not spared.

My mother truly reflected the forgiving and second chance nature of God in my childhood, after facing repercussions for my actions she sat me on her lap. I immediately started looking for Ashton Kutcher, I had to be getting punked! When I sat on her lap crying she said to me what she ALWAYS say after I test her patience, "Nodia there is nothing you can ever do that will make me love you less, But I don't care if I have to fight you for you as long as you're with me you better do the right thing". I was so happy. My mother loved me even when she corrected me and moments like those have been instrumental in our relationship. The next day when I woke up I was happy, cause at least I could still change my clothes.

MOMMA SAYS:
"You can have a boyfriend when you go to high-school"
"You can have a boyfriend when you Get your high school diploma"
You can have a boyfriend when you start to settle down in your college studies.
You can have a boyfriend after you have completed your 4 years and get your degree

You can have a boyfriend once I know that you have become a well-rounded young woman and have academic success along with an airtight relationship with Christ and model's positive behavior to the children of the church while pursuing your own success and evolving every day.

These are the stages to the simple question I've asked my mother my entire childhood- adolescence and even in young adulthood. "When Can I Have a boyfriend?" She'd always ask why? Sex Duhhh. So, I'd go down the list from "I just want a friend who I can talk to" to "I know my limits and I have self-control" and eventually reach "Do you want me to be an old maid the rest of my life?!"

There're still things that my mother has never found out about my idiot days in junior high and I truly believe with all my heart that when I prayed and asked God to hide it from her, he did. Nothing gets past that lady unless I ask God to hold me down. She knew everything but a big part of it was that she chose her battles. I got in trouble a lot growing up and sometimes the repercussions were great and others I would get a pass. She always said, "I expect you to be teenager because that's what you are" and that was what helped me get out of some sticky situations. In 8th grade I decided I would date a high school boy because they were more mature (Thank Jesus for my praying mother). When the news broke in the family and she was coming to talk to me I felt as if I were in 7th grade all over again. She sat on the bed and said, "So you have a boyfriend", I said, "I had a boyfriend, but I already broke up with him" Mom said "Okay, Love You, see you after I come back from church". Ya girl had gotten away with MURDER and I was soooo happy that I got back with my boyfriend the very next day.

He was a dark skinned, 5'4 10th grader who lived in the projects, had no money, no goals, gang banging, sweet talking, pants at his knees 10th grader. Just the way I liked them (Thank Jesus for

Deliverance). Even after mommy demonstrated trust in her baby girl, I still got back with my boo. Here is how I know she casted a spell on me. I felt super guilty and super paranoid. I remember hanging out and doing what any stupid, unprepared pre-teens in relationships do, KISSING. Kissing in the park in the projects on a dirty bench, in the projects. Can we pause a minute to talk about how much I didn't know what I was doing, I mean there was saliva all across my face. Anyways getting "felt up" was just as uncomfortable to me as the words look paired together. Having some strange boy hands on me felt uncomfortable. You know that boyfriend you have that you always feel guilty with and you know exactly how bad he is for you but you still with him, yeah well that was me at 13. Remember when I said I was unprepared? it was for a reason because I was not ready for what he did next. All of sudden I felt this foreign touch heading in the direction of my Lady Jewels. YALL. I shut that down faster than a prison during a riot. After Dramatically exiting the park I called my more experienced friend to get the info on what exactly this high schooler was trying to do. When I found out, I broke up with him, for good. Momma was always right, I wasn't ready for boys.

Many times after that scenario I would get in trouble again, it was not the end of my rebellion. Looking back at my turbulent yet passionate relationship with my mother it makes sense why we are still so close. It is because regardless of the storms we weathered, we braced them TOGETHER. She did not expose my misfortunes, but she covered them. Our present-day relationship to the outside world will most likely look like a fairytale and that's because it is. We overcame ourselves and our struggle, we stuck it out, and though "teeth and tongue may meet" meaning that because we are close we will inevitably bump heads sometimes, we have learned the art of listening and apologizing. It was never easy, and I can't guarantee that you reading this will have an easy experience with your parent but seek the infinite wisdom of God on those issues and while you wait on your answer, "whatsoever is pure, true, and honest, think on it". I had no patience, I didn't want guidance, I wanted to figure things out on my own. Better yet, I thought I already had it figured out. There was this mindset that "it will never be me" as if I was untouchable. I wasn't untouchable, I wasn't invincible. But I dived in anyways. Into a life that maximized your flaws and minimized your potential. A life that took you places and never bothered to bring you back. A life that swallows you whole. Make no mistake, that life was my choice. I was always a rather impatient child always wanting things done and executed quickly. The fast life bedazzled me, not because I was naïve to the danger, but because safety was all I've ever known. With safety came curiosity so I did what any girl my age do I decided that it was time to do things my way. If being the girl that I wanted to be was not allowed, then I would go somewhere where I can be her. Everything I did was scrutinized, everything I did had judgment, everything I did had a punishment and it was all because I was the main attraction, so no more would I sit with crossed legs in the front, no more would I be on the stage but I would retreat behind the curtain to become that girl mama told me that I shouldn't ever be.

CLOSED CURTAINS

My life had become a façade placated with false assurances of men who wore me on their sleeves and kept their heart in the bottom of their boots.

It was safe to say that momma's little girl was all grown up now.

My body was a temple, open for any self-loathing, insidious, narcissistic broken piece of a man to enter in.

I was prepared to offer myself as a sacrifice, a lamb to be slaughtered for the greater good.

I gave men pieces of me that belonged to me.

Soon enough the essence of my character took shelter in my shadow and they both lived behind the scenes...

Don't you hate sitting in the front row at church? I know I did. It was so intimidating and stressful. Legs crossed, smile always, modesty is policy, sleeping not allowed, and not to mention the various times that you must shout hallelujah or break into a praise dance to avoid looking sinful. Growing up as a child of a pastor didn't afford me the privilege of being myself, it only brought me disdain and judgements. I was extra-scrutinized with the standards of an orthodox nun. Most times I felt as if the church wanted me to be more perfect than my mother, as if the only way they can feel assured of their future success is to dictate mine. The pressure to be perfect made me feel so low that I started getting high off risky behavior and promiscuity. I lived for hidden hallways in the sanctuary where Christians and their kids alike took a break from righteousness and engaged in sin full throttle. The stage that religion placed us on would always send us off running backstage. As any addict my tolerance for sin grew and skipping service in the back or flirting with church musicians was not enough. I decided I would live my life behind the curtain. The first time I decided on consensual sex I was 19 and I figured its nothing worth saving anymore. At 18 years old I was date-raped by a guy I was friends with, for lack of a better word. It was the day I was pinned in high school as a dental assistant. I remember getting out of school early and normally I would have to go straight home, but today was pinning. The ceremony started at 5pm and I probably got out around 2:45pm. The extra time in between was already assigned to be spent with a guy friend of mine. I went over his house not naïve to what might happen but unprepared to how far he may have wanted it to go. He had been a family friend for a long time and it was a long-developed crush that was never explored so I figured everything would be okay. I figured wrong. Things got physical fairly quickly and the more it progressed the more I resisted. Still unaware to what was to come, though I felt uncomfortable I didn't feel unsafe. I mean this guy was practically family. He got up and said he needed to go to the bathroom, to use it is what I assumed. When he came back my discerning spirit told me something was different, I ignored it. I pushed passed my feelings and said nothing. A few moments later I felt a tugging at my jeans. "Whatever" I thought to myself, but I got an awful ache in my stomach, I knew I had to stop. My mother's words ambushed me right in that very moment and I said "no". He kept going. I said, "can we stop?". "Please stop", "I gotta go", "I'm not trying to do this right now". I guess I was too subtle. Soon my repetitive reproach was answered with a "Shut up". An indescribable numbness came over as I used my hands trying to block what was happening to me. My life began to flash before my eyes, "is this my story?", I laid there a witness to my death as he killed my innocence. When he had finished, he let my hands go. As I walked back into the school I felt a million eyes looking at me, funny thing is, no one was there. I walked to the bathroom and called my friend Mo. She patched me up so that I would be able to receive my award. I would later find out That day, the boy who I would later fall in love with pointed me out to his mom and Identified me as the girl he would marry. That day, I stood on stage as my mom cheered me on for being the top student in that class. That day, I told one person. I still hadn't been calling what happened to me rape because I went over, I was sending all the sexy text messages, it was my fault. That one person told me it wasn't my fault. I needed to hear that. It helped, but I didn't heal, I was wounded. I went to church of course, feeling unfixable but still performing because it was second nature to me. So, there I was at 19 with the boy I loved, and I figured, "why the hell not?", "there is nothing to save anymore!" "It's just stupid holding back something that had no value anymore". So, I did it. I had sex. The more I had sex the more I hated myself, my personal conviction about pre-marital sex made me very depressed about the fact that I still was doing it no matter how remorseful. I jumped into that relationship fairly quickly after the abuse and it caused me to suffer with severe PTSD throughout the relationship. On and off for the next five to six years I spent countless hours questioning my boyfriend's fidelity, going through our conversations with a fine-toothed comb looking for a fault in him. Mama was right "I wasn't ready". During that relationship I fought against anxiety, depression and even suicidal thoughts. However, I held it together so well that the poor guy never even noticed. The PLOT THICKENS. To add to my spiritual conviction, my moral conviction was also in play because I was not allowed to date. So, between playing hide and seek with God and my mother I began to feel overwhelmed. My affection and affirmations of love decreased day by day, not only to the boyfriend I wasn't supposed to have but to my FAMILY. I could no longer look people in the eye. I didn't like kissing. I hesitated to say, "I love you". I developed a huge anger problem. I experienced multiple anxiety attacks a week. Lastly, I didn't love myself. As time went on, I began to resent my boyfriend for wanting sex like any other young man his age because the only difference I seen between him and my aggressor was that he loved me, and I didn't believe that was enough to keep him from hurting me; mostly because I didn't believe I was lovable in the first place. After leaving that relationship for what now seems like a small issue I decided to work on myself. Isn't that what all women do after a breakup?

Well I "tried" to work on myself is a better and more honest choice of words. Most of my days were spent trying to cleanse myself of the night before and most of the nights were spent creating a person that needed to be cleansed. I was in a CYCLE and a dangerous one too.

The funny thing about cycles is that most times you're unaware that you are even in one. I had no idea that I had entered a viscous cycle of negative self-worth and sin. Life behind the scenes felt better than ever. I was living on my own terms. You know you've done it before. Yes you. Shout out that you're living your best life while suffering in silence. "Fighting without and fears within" like the Baptists would say. One thing I know for sure is that behind the curtains felt secure. It was the security I searched for since for a while I felt unsafe. Most people recover from a situation by entering into another, no matter how unsafe. For me this statement was oh so very true.

Girls will be girls.

The crash of my relationship left me open myself to a sepulcher of men, and I wasn't complaining. It had become a medicine to me. No strings, no stress! I met a guy, and he was Fiiineeeeeeeeeeeeeee. I mean fine. Smooth buttery skin, Tall, Just the right amount of muscle, great smile and ALLAT. I met him at a party. Me and my girls were passing a backyard and got invited to the party for free while on our way to another fiesta. We figured "why not?" I mean who turns down free entry? The three of us had on dresses, one violet-blue stretch fit open back that hugged my curves and did EVERYTHAANGGG for my figure yall, another in a black trendy mini dress that showed her slender legs and lastly an animal print bodycon for the most untamed in the group, we did not come to play! There he was, standing at about 6"2 sipping on his drink eye-ing me. The more he eyed the more I gave him something to look at. After several glances he grabbed my hand and pulled me out of the party to somewhere quiet. JUST TAKE A MOMENT TO REALIZE HOW I AM MAKING THIS SOUND SLIGHTLY ROMANTIC, THAT'S PERSPECTIVE. He asked me my name and inquired about where I lived, we sat there the entire night and talked about what we do, what we like to do and even got into the famous conversation that all-party people have which is "I don't really party because there's nothing to get from it, it's just something to do". I left the party that night not feeling like I had found love but like I had found the perfect person to take my mind off life. Two days later, he came over.

I was so excited about him coming over for several reasons. I thought that having a man was the answer. I figured having someone to call me pretty, take me out and rub on me was what I needed to feel happy, notice how love is not in there. I wanted someone around because being alone with my demons were much too haunting. I wanted sex because that was the closest I ever got to receiving love from a man. Momma was right, I wasn't ready. At such a young age all you will ever think about is what you want. What about what you are willing to give? Baby you have so much inside of you that you need to discover, so much untapped potential, you are not even aware of what you have to offer. Ask yourself, what do I have to give to a significant other? What can the person give to me? Can this person pour into my purpose? Will they recognize the divine call on my life? Am I financially, spiritually, mentally and even physically capable of loving them the way that they receive love? Is it love, or is it Codependency? Will we be able to entwine our God given purpose not only for a healthy, love filled, fruitful, great sex, adventurous, spontaneous, spirit filled, empowering marriage but one that will further lift the kingdom of God and lead to his glorification? Not only that are you ready for baggage? Becoming one with someone infers that what was theirs is yours too. No longer me, but now us. Are you ready to share your demons? Is your relationship with God on a level that will equip you to slay the dragons of the one you love? As a man have you ever considered the number of women that are sexually abused and assaulted? Your wife may be one of them. Do you take time to consider that you might trigger her if you ask for sex? Do you even know what a trigger is?

The dynamics of love and relationship is one that requires the understanding of one's self and the experience of God's love. Truly when you have known and felt the sensation and sweet caress of true love, then and only then will you be able to dispense it. Oh? Yall thought this book was only about Jesus? **It is**, Just another perspective.

Through His Eyes

Remember a little while ago when I hinted on perspectives? Well it's important that you have some of your own. When you read my story the guy at the party sounded like a nice guy, but not because you knew him, met him, or seen him but because it was the picture that I painted. Think back or even turn the page back. I gave you no details of his character I just described what I was feeling. A lot of times we are in sticky situations because we only see things from one perspective, whether it be what someone told us, what we felt, or what we think we saw. I later on found out the importance of perspective too when I found myself with that same guy's hands around my neck choking me in an effort to show me who's boss. We had only been talking for a week when I thought I should let him know that he cannot tell me what to do or say. Sort of seductive like a snake his hands creeped up to my collarbone and made its way around my neck and before I knew it I could not find air. Sometimes looking at our lives through the lens of Christ may be painful but one thing for sure is that what we will behold, is true. If I had took time to use the sight that God gave me I would have sensed the danger that felt like comfort. All because of a perspective. I wasn't looking with the eye that God gave me. That eye had long closed, because with it, even behind the curtain, it exposed my nakedness.

Let It All Hang Out

The story of Adam and Eve took placed so many decades ago, yet I can perfectly relate to it in my world today. I mean come on a man and A woman get everything they ever wanted but they still want more. Like I said before it's something about safety that just makes you curious. When Adam and eve partook of the forbidden fruit they immediately began to see things in a different perspective. See we don't realize that having the ability to see means that we would see our own imperfections. As soon as Adam and Eve realized that they were naked they began to Cover themselves with the leaves in the garden. They were naked their entire existence, but this one act changed everything can't you relate? How often do you see One thing change our entire life? Well my thing was sex. I mean I'm saying it like I was swinging from chandeliers which is not the case but for me it was life changing. The plan was one guy, but there wasn't one guy. The choice had been snatched and I had believed that I didn't have the power to choose anymore. But, by all means let me not paint a picture that the entire time it was about the rape because it wasn't. It was about me. It was about the ability it had to make me feel like I had value. Believe me when I say it didn't make me feel priceless but that didn't matter as long as I wasn't worthless. Sex is the confirmation of love and the evidence of attraction. It exposes vulnerability and creates a connection that cannot be seen with the naked eye. It is the giving of yourself to someone else. The reason I have felt so downtrodden about premarital sex is because I place it in high regards. To be that vulnerable means to put yourself at risk for hurt. When you kiss someone are you thinking about only the gratification of it or the fact that your lips is a blessing lol! If you think of your body as blessing, then it would be easier for you to refrain from those who haven't earned it. Like Nicki Minaj says "You gotta be king status to get in my body…". And that is for men and women, boys and girls, everyone! You won't find any double standards here OKAY! Back to what I was saying, sex starts in the mind. The conception of a thought, the thought of simply a kiss. Would it be weird if I told you Kissing someone means you may want to have sex with them? Am I making sense? I feel like I'm losing you! Lemme Explain.

If you buy a gun, you should expect that you may have to shoot, if you shoot there is a possibility that you may kill.

I'm trying to explain that sex is the last step in a chain of events that started earlier than you thought. So, for people who are trying to remain virgins or maintain celibacy monitor your body's reactions and notice when you've taken the first step. I mean cause me personally I can't kiss forever baby something's gotta give! For all those appalled at my sexual content this is PG-13 compared to Songs of Solomon, cut it out.

Breaking those soul ties was hard but you know what was harder, curbing the appetite, oh lawd! Have I gone too far? I don't think so. A lot of people try things like pornography and masturbation to curb cravings because they want to stay celibate but baby I got news for you it's kinda sex still. Christians always trying to invent ways to sneak in a little bit of sex, my people crack me up! The root of kicking the craving and I'm not saying it's going to go away completely because we are sexual beings, HELLO! We tend to look a sex in this animalistic and perverted way and really SEX IS DIVINE. Pornography is teaching our kids that sex is this foot up in the air, arch in ya back, name calling, physically turbulent thing, which is the case for some (don't knock it till you try it) BUT it's so prevalent that sex has become casual. When the creator said be fruitful and multiply it didn't have to be a pleasurable thing, but it is, so I like to think that gratification from sex is a gift. Thank ya Lord! Putting all my crazy talk aside, get to understand the true value of yourself and the giving of yourself. Remember that in exposing yourself you are leaving your entire being and soul and open to someone all while creating a tie that's difficult to break, and not everyone deserves that part of you.

The hardest thing is not to take the risk, the hardest thing is to choose which risk to take. I mean, before I had no regard or thought process on my body but now, oh lewd. After the first date I have already practice your last name on the end of mines, decided whether I'd take your name or hyphenate, chosen the house, worked out how many arguments I would take the loss for, name our children, chosen the wedding flowers (definitely orchids), and most importantly worked out whether I want to marry you at all. I know it's a little weird to someone that I have decided if I want to marry someone based on the first date, sounds a little crazy honestly. I believe that if you look there would be signs of potential benefactors and hazards in the future, even on the first date. Does he/she consider you? I went on a little date the other day and the guy was meeting me at 6am I thought it was amazing that he brought me a bottle of water. It wasn't any special water, but it was the thought. I thought to myself it's early he's probably tired and he was rushing to meet me, but I crossed his mind and he felt that I should be hydrated. Sounds silly right? Look at the little things that someone does. I didn't see it as he cared about me so much because we just met, but it showed me his character, I thought that was profound. There are signs that can warn us of future issues or hint us on a magical future just look. There is one thing that can cloud that sight and it's that Humping baby! You ever like somebody but not nothing serious you just think they're cool and as soon as you have sex with them they automatically become the next best thing? That's your judgement being clouded. Of course, they get extra brownie points for tickling your fancy. Sex slows down the process of actually getting to know someone. It is the one thing that can allow you to miss what's there and see what's not, that's how powerful it is. Make sure you have a good idea of who someone is before getting physical Don't hop on the sex train without expecting to eventually end up at Baby Central Station. Remember the example I gave about the gun, it's all a chain reaction. All in all, seek divine guidance, you'll know what's right.

PIMPS, PARTIES AND PRAYER

Let the sun shine in on your soul
close the windows of your mind and open the doors of your heart
you are invincible
your brown eyes are the fire of the earth
soar like an eagle
live as unconcerned as a babe
hands folded mantis like always steadfast in prayer
and run as fast as you can
and smash into **YOURSELF.**

"Girl you look good, won't you back that thang up, you a big fine woman won't you back that thang up" As the timeless hit ran through the speakers, I shook what my momma gave me. And My outfit, Girl, it would've made a stripper blush. That was the objective, to take someone home rather than to be taken home. The eye shadow that took me 15 minutes to apply with my index finger had started to disappear from the sweat that covered my face and my 4B hair texture had already began to show its colors and misbehave. All different shades, textures, and characters of men approached me claiming to be of pure intentions which honestly didn't matter to me. Some were betrothed, and some were not, many were red flags, but a guy wrapped in caution tape would still get my number if he said the right thing. I mean I was broken what do you expect? The goal simply was to find a man, become his idea of the perfect woman, spend his money and discard him when he messes up, which he will. It was all too easy because at a party no one is looking for commitment anyways. Partying was the long sought-after antidote to my depression, but it was temporary. It only lasted as long as my hangover. Before 21

I already had preferred choice of liquor and acquired a taste for vodka and nights that you don't remember in the morning. It was a cycle. Party, Pass Out, Morning Hangovers, followed by severe crying episodes, a short prayer and hymn, quick sex wherever I could find it, Shower and head to the Party. REPEAT. In spite of the life I decided to dive into I never missed one Sunday of church. I went sometimes straight from the party. **I knew that was where my Healing was, I just wasn't ready to address the pain.** I always knew God's address just didn't quite build up the strength to visit. I felt as if I had to get a couple things in order first. It was until later realized that I needed to relinquish my right to receive God's restoration. We all have the right to fix things in our lives, god granted that gift to us. However, when we refuse to acknowledge that he is the source of our strength our efforts towards righteousness become in vain. A hymn that is well loved in my congregation goes…

"Invain thou strugglest to get free, I never will unloose the hold, art thou the man that died for me, the secret of the love unfold, wrestling I will not let thee go, until thy name and nature know"

Meaning that many times we fight against the right thing but with the wrong mentality, so our efforts are equivalent to pelting blows at the wind. God never lets us go even though we distance ourselves from him and unveiling that secret to ourselves and accepting that his love is truly unconditional will empower you with the strength you need to evolve through trials and press towards self-actualization.

Don't be fooled…

My experiences have left scars on my character but spiced up my personality, added to my wisdom and gifted me the spirit of prayer in a way that I will be forever grateful for. Prayer to me always felt like vain repetition growing up and that's because it was. My religion's general prayer style consisted of reciting hymns and bible scriptures, I have come to accept and loved that prayer style because sometimes it fills the gap for a believer who doesn't know what to say. However, it is important to not have a prayer that your church, kids, partner, parents and the devil himself may have already memorized. I once heard a Spiritual Elder Teacher Kester Baptiste say that Baptist people say the same thing in prayer they don't know how to romance God, it made me think. My growth in prayer came about different to most kingdom builders. My prayer life was enriched through my sin, believe it or not. When you're a bad child you got to come up with new ways to appease and get the attention of your father. **Sin in the mind is a hindrance and sin in action is rebellious, but sin completed is a lesson.** One that can cultivate, equip, and propel you to another dimension and that is how my sin helped my prayer life. Think about it this way Prayer is Presentation. You step into the room, introduce yourself, compliment the audience or company, share your knowledge of them and as soon as they're buttered up to you, hit them with the proposal! After it is only a matter of thanking them for their time and expressing to them how much you are looking forward to their favorable answer. Try that with your prayer life. Make a presentation that cannot be turned down, one that will get you that promotion you've been eyeing, or the raise. So, there I was, praying more, attending all services and events, cleaning the sanctuary, paying my tithes and all! I had accepted sin as something I couldn't overcome and attempted to mask the guilt with righteous acts. Soon enough the curtain that I hid behind opened up. Annnnnnddddddddddd ACTION!

My cousin Angel came back super excited with the news that she had met some great guy at the corner store while buying pads. I lived in the hood, you don't meet great guys at the corner store while buying pads. My cousin was a very bubbly character. She wasn't naïve, just too brave. So, her and a good friend of mine Pearl came back to the house singing praises of the corner store pad man. Already claiming him to be kind, chivalrous and husband material. I mean it seemed to me that these ladies were swooped off their feet. As they continue to tell me and my best friend Michelle about the corner store pad man. I wasn't in the mood, it had only been a couple days since I had an abusive encounter with a guy I was talking to. I caught Michelle up while they were at the corner store, so she was less interested in the story and more concerned with nursing me back to health. These two just kept going. Between flashbacks of the abuse and a show that I was watching I heard "he invited us to go party with him tonight, He said he'll pay for everything". I calmly passed on the invitation with the obvious reason of we don't know him. As they began to try to convince me of how great of an opportunity this was, I got irritated. Pearl was saying "it's not every day you get to turnup for free", Angel followed up with "he was really nice, and mad cool". The more they talked the more irritated I became but their nagging had nothing on the voices in my head, so I decided "whatever, we don't got nothing to do tonight anyways and its free". Big mistake. We got dolled up for what almost felt like a blind date. Waiting outside I pointed out that we might be waiting for a psycho killer and convinced the girls that we wait down the street instead of directly in front of my house. When the taxi pulled up it was a Latino man in a suit, probably mid-thirties, with glasses and a ring on each hand, José. We got in the car and a night we won't forget began. Jose's friend was the driver, we all sat in the back seat having conversation with Jose and his friend on our way to the first event. Something didn't feel right. As we pulled up to the party everyone nerves began to react, not because we were with a stranger, we were worried the party might be boring. While walking Jose looked at me and said, "you're so beautiful, come walk with me", I complied. He asked Pearl too. There we were with a stranger walking into a party on both arms of Jose. The party sucked. It was 50th birthday bash and we looked like escorts, I felt like one to be honest. We told Jose we weren't feeling it and so we left. As we walked out the door we figured our night was over, we tried and failed, and it was time to go home. "Damnnn, that was mad wack!" Jose said. "It got a couple other things moving tonight though, yall wanna come". I said no in my mind. We got in the car and was on our way to spot number two. Now Jose had taken a liking to me, according to him I was exactly his type, Great. Not only was I out with a creep, but the creep liked me. I wasn't even at the corner store! We walked into party number two which at first sight was definitely going to be a bust. The girls walked ahead, and I behind cuffed to the arm of Jose. This party had security, I thought "wow, this is ghetto". The girls were already inside when the guard stretched out his hand to Jose. He bent over and pulled a gun from his shoe and gave it to the guard. The corner store pad man had a gun. I kept it to myself, I didn't want to scare the girls, I was always motherly in that way. Jose's friend ordered a bottle of Cîroc that after a short girl meeting we all had decided we were not drinking, except Angel. "It's sealed" she said. As if the worst thing that could happen to us was getting drunk and being hungover the next morning. After a few more stern no's, angel took our advice and replied, "well I'm taking it home, we'll drink it later". Party number two was just as boring as party number one so we left. By this time Michelle was irritated and ready to go home and started telling Jose that he was wack and she was ready to go, quite the firecracker she is. I decided it was time to tell her about the gun, I thought it would make her shut up, I was wrong. On the ride to party number three I had already pictured three different scenarios of how the night would end and they all ended with someone dead. When we arrived at the third spot it was a house. We entered through the backyard. We walked in a side door and there were only men in what looked like a home-built bar I counted about twenty of them, but there was one woman. A black woman with a blonde wig, her makeup looked like her kids had drawn on her face, she was high. The sleeping and don't fall kind of high. For a minute she looked at me and I wasn't sure if she was conscious, but it felt like I could hear her warning me to turn around. We kept walking. Through the crowd, down the stairs into a small room. There were more men. The small room held about twenty more guys. It was covered in black writing all over, smoke clouded the room, there was no chairs, there was no music, just men and us. One man sat on a crate just looking at us and I knew this is where our story ended. "Oh hell no we need to dip NOWWWW" Michelle saved the day. God saved our lives. While walking out again I looked for the woman, she was gone. Michelle continued to complain telling Jose to take us home. At this point we were all pretty shaken up. Pearl figured it out, he was a pimp. She said she had seen one before and Jose showed all the signs. We were ready to go but now too scared to speak up. On to spot number four, Club Temptations. It was about two in the morning when we got to temptations. The body guard had to be bribed to let us in seeing that we were all under aged. Jose ended up borrowing money from his very angry friend to get us in. When we walked in it was packed, people everywhere and music was blasting. Immediately we all got on the dance floor ready to forget everything that happened earlier. After about two songs I felt a firm hand hold me and pulled me from among the crowd, Jose. He started talking to me about his last relationship, showing me pictures of basically an Instagram model, she was stunning and obviously out of his league. After the melodrama of his past he began telling me how much he wants to take me out. I wondered "where is the gun?". The rest of the night Jose hung onto my every move, I watched my girls dancing and cheered them on from the sidelines, hooked on the arm of the pimp for the rest of the night. The party was ending, the lights had been turned on and the night had ended pretty well considering the previous events. We began walking to the car, it was pretty cold outside, and we were not dressed for the weather. As we waited for Jose and his friend to catch up I felt safe enough to let all the girls know about the gun. "What the f*** is wrong with yall?" we stood there in shock as Jose yelled at us. "Don't yall ever leave my f****** side when we out, yall are with me, I'm taking care of yall!". I knew it, this was our end. Apparently, Michelle didn't care she started yelling back "who the hell are you talking to? You aint my man or my daddy!". As we told her to calm down we all got in the car and decided it was best nothing was said. It was agreed, we would do what was necessary to get home. Along the drive Jose's friend decided he didn't want to take us home anymore, so we had to catch a cab. Jose decided to take us home to pay for the cab, but while hooked on his arm I remembered he had no money left, what he did have was a gun. As we sat in the car I mentally prepared myself for the life of a prostitute and had already decided I have to protect Michelle at all cost she was the youngest. As we approached the block I seen the face of the blonde hair woman, I told the cab to stop "we'll get out right here" I said. Jose said it was no problem, he'll drop us in front the house, but I refused as I pushed the girls out the car. "who's paying?" the cab driver asked. I knew we had to hurry. As we said our goodbyes Jose took our fake numbers so that we could hang out again, he made a date with each one of us for different days of the week. As the car drove off I seen it make a right, he was coming around the block. "If yall don't get to the house when I'm there you will be locked out" was the last thing I said before I began sprinting towards the house. It was the fastest I've ever ran in my life, the girls knew I was serious, they were right behind me. When we got inside I decide to tell angel and pearl what happened to me earlier that week and we agreed to never do that again. The next morning Angel walked in the room laughing attempting to show us something on her phone. It was a text from Jose. "You gave him your real number?" I asked angrily. "I didn't know we were giving fake ones" angel said. I shook my head. Girls will be Girls...

Friends...

For as long as I could remember I had wanted them. It seems as if life had been always trying to teach me that "everyone is not your friend". So long I've been afraid of sharing how I felt afraid of hurting someone else. Protecting them but crippling me. But this book is not about me. It's about you. So, take a look into a personal letter I wrote to my friend.

Dear friend,

It seems as if time has flown by from since we were young and dumb and reckless. I look at you and I see someone but it's no one I can recognize and yes that should be good, but your transformation has only seemed to drive a wedge between us. I think about us and everything we've been through and there is so much that can be said and done but there seems to be one reoccurring question that occupies my brain and it is "was it ever real?". Now I don't mean to come off possessive, but I thought what we had was special. I listened to you carefully recount the ways in which I "hurt" you and I checked the dates. Does it mean that you have held me in your heart for all that time and not in the loving way. In the way that serial killers do, or a woman scorned would behave. It scared me to know that I had been laying my head on the bosom of a person who could've killed me. To know that I had been breathing life into a person who envied mine. And now I just recount our special moments to see if I can spot the imperfections in your love for me, and in every person, I see your betrayal, and in every friend, I feel Your deception. You left me for friends who sucked the life I breathed into you. You left me for a love that was unpredictable, and you wanted a part of me that you were supposed to give yourself. Why did you let people come between us? Why did you take all of me without intentions to share yourself? I think for me it has always been the same, but I didn't allow myself to see it. I was so afraid of being alone. So afraid of starting over. As our paths began to shift into separate directions I followed you hoping that we could still walk as a team, but it was behind you that I realized we are not the same. We never were. Our emptiness created a space that we so desperately wanted to fill with each other. And it became hazardous to our futures. So, I accept it. I accept that it is over. I will no longer chase happily never afters and maybes. Instead I wish you the best. If our paths were to meet again I know that it will be ten times the friendship we have already. I understand that I am being positioned for something I don't understand and if that position is away from you I have decided to trust my creator. So, as you walk in your lane, walk with your head held high and become great, that's still the plan, though I'm not in your lane I'll be cheering you on from mine.

Until next time dear friend….

They never got it.

I remember when I thought friends were a requirement, turns out they're a blessing and privilege. You'll be lucky to have one good friend if any. Since learning that friends can break your heart worse than lovers, ya girl has been extra cautious. I remember one day I took the last of my money and bought flowers for two of my friends. I wanted to show them that they were special and that no man should ever drop their panties for nothing regular. I showed my mom with so much excitement before leaving the house, but she seemed so worried. She was scared. She didn't want her baby girl to exert herself to the point of no return. I never did stop doing things like that because its who I am and though one of those relationships may be estranged it hasn't changed me. I will always choose to the stand in the integrity of who I am in any relationship, your distance will not change me. I choose not to give anyone that power instead I will respond accordingly to whatever is presented. It is important to remember who you want to be in every situation. NOT WHO YOU ARE BUT WHO YOU WANT TO BE! Cause let's face it most of us are not at the place in life where we let arrogant and hurtful behavior slide but if we remember what we are aspiring to be, it keeps us aligned. EYES ON THE PRIZE. Besides, I had way too much going on to be stuck on someone else, HELLO.

S-E-X and all of the above

As much friend and familial problems, I had I couldn't give them my full attention because I had real life man problems yall. You know what it is to live wounded but not be dead? That was me. Despite walking around like everything was fine I was wounded. I had soul ties that I had no idea how to break. I didn't have to have sex with a lot of people either. I've wanted to have sex since I knew what it was I'm just fast like that, but when I was abused, and the decision was taken from me sex became everything it was not supposed to be. It became the means by which I forgot my issues and it was temporal satisfaction that made me feel valued. Sex is supposed to be this awesome binding experience in its most simple definition. I thought that if I didn't care then there would be no binding but that wasn't true. I was acting liked the men I hardly knew. I was stuck in areas that I had mastered previously, and I had changed. I was so ashamed, not of the actual sexual activity but of the little value I placed on it. You see to me if I kept the value I had for sex intact after what happened to me then it would only shed light on how screwed up I actually am. So, to cope with those feelings I made sex casual, it was no longer a big deal. I took on that mindset even in a relationship and to hide that reality I pretended that sex was still important even though my actions were not congruent.

Sex is so taboo for Christians that I fear I've already shared too much. But who cares right? It's not about them. Sex is awesome but with the right person at the right time. Do you want to give yourself to prematurely? No. Listen my standards are marriage, I have no idea what yours are but "take my stupid advice" as my grandmother would say, get some standards and stick to them. Not for anyone else but for you. Standards gives you value and an idea of self-worth. You know recently I've been thinking about why we place so much value on sex. Have you ever thought about it why sex is so important to you? In my kingdom journey I recognized that I wanted sex to feel valued. That wasn't what it was for. So, I became celibate because I knew that while I was emotionally unstable it wouldn't manifest as beautifully as it should. It's crazy how I'm talking about it right? I speak with this tone because that's what it is. Listen I'm trying to swing from chandeliers and allat! I'm just making sure the next time ya girl ties up herself to someone, it's with someone who has baggage I'm willing and ready to handle and vice versa. So yes, the sex is great but what else are they bringing to the table? Yes, it makes you feel better, but does it solve the problem? And don't let anyone pressure you love. Get someone who values themselves, so they regard you in that same way. I often hear "get a man who treats his mother well, or a woman that can take care of a house", while it does reveal some vital signs of a person's character nothing shows me how they will value me more than how much they value themselves. Some people find it easy to take care of others and value the people around them. If they don't love themselves and you tie yourself to them and become one, he will treat you like he treat himself. REMEMBER you are NOT his mama! You are NOT her house! Do not base your sole decision off of how they are treating a totally different situation unless you plan to conform to it. So, unless you plan to treat him like your son don't expect him to treat you like his mama, and unless you plan to become an inanimate object don't expect her to treat you like one. Walk in wisdom, young grasshopper.

BAG LADY

I could feel it.
The exhaustion. The Pain. The Regret. The Brokenness. The Shame.
I could feel her slipping away with every failed attempt to find you.
Carrying the baggage of her scattered past, abominable present
and terrifying future. I held contempt in my hands, abuse on my
shoulders, the devil on my back and depression and anxiety sat
in my back pockets. It wasn't the truth of my life that held me
back, it was the lie of the serpent that told me God's word was
not true. It crippled me and when angels hovered and stirred the
pool of my existence I refrained from the healing because who I
was couldn't be erased. I escaped my aggressors, but I couldn't let
go of my decisions. How could I be so stupid?

"Bag Lady, you gon hurt your back, dragging all them bags
like that" …
"One day all them bags, gon get in your way".
-Erykah Badu

Time have seemed to have flown by since I can remember my morphological change into the being I am today. Ever since I can remember I was a happy child. I was so blessed I didn't even know how poor I was. I thought me, and 9 other family members shared a studio basement apartment because we loved each other, I thought when my GRANDMOTHER mixed flour and water to stick pictures on my science projects that she was just creative. I was naïve, innocent and blind to the turmoil's in my life and I didn't care because I was happy. I was the kid who thought they had it all, always talking too much and laughing too hard. I still remember my mom saying, "little girls must be seen and not heard". I was opinionated, bold and brave. I was the leader, the smart girl and the girl everyone couldn't help but love. As I grew up I lived life being an easy person to please, in love with nature and appreciating the small things in life, but when the reality of life hit me I became weak and fragile. I stood in the mirror and stared at myself, I hardly recognized the reflection. I was never weak nor fragile. I tried to pinpoint when everything changed and what exact moment caused this turn in my life. Was it after I was honored for being the top dental assistant in my class, when I was Date-raped by a longtime family friend. I remember as I stood on the stage to accept my award with everyone cheering me on and telling me how proud they were to see me accomplish that much in high school. He stole my innocence, my virginity, my freedom of choice. Was that my turning point? Or could it have been the second time being sexually and physically abused by another "friend". I mean, surely being choked out can change a person, but I was still me. I was a depressed, self-pitying, suicidal, damaged version of myself, but nevertheless still me. I sat in front of the computer busting my brain thinking could it have been the surgery that left me with one ovary. Nope it wasn't that either. Could it have been my childhood trauma? Could it have been the abuse I suffered at the hands of a friend's brother? I looked at the mirror then back at the computer and couldn't remember how I became this person. All of a sudden it hit me like a ton of bricks, it was the day I tried to take my life. Things had been so hard after all the abuse and partying and trying to get back my mother's trust was harder than I thought. She had no idea the extent of the life that I lived while out of her care. She was going on a business trip. I was instructed not to go to Pearl's birthday party while she was gone. I was okay with it until I was at home watching the events through social media. It was late, I was alone and then the thoughts began. Flashbacks of the abuse, of the trauma flooded my brain. I needed a drink and not the one underneath the kitchen sink. I needed a drink from pearl's party, so I went. As expected and anticipated my mother found out, I didn't care. She was so upset, I didn't expect it. As she went

48

on and on about my punishment and what a disappointment I was, the thought creeped into my mind. "End it". I decided I am going to end it. I walked into the bathroom and locked the door. "Shit, we have a walk-in shower not a tub". I had no idea how the suicide thing worked. "Forget it" I thought. I got in the shower. Those flashbacks came back. I took the blade and slightly ran it across my wrist, "shit, this hurts!". I began slightly running it a couple more times trying to close my eyes in between and make a real cut, I couldn't do it. I sank to the floor and began to cry "I couldn't even kill myself". My mom busted in the bathroom and pulled open the shower curtain, looking like she was seeing the second coming of Christ. "What the hell is wrong with you Nodia? You wanna kill yourself? Then you must be crazy? I'm calling the ambulance to take you!". It was a little late for the drama scene I had already changed my mind. After several attempts I convinced her that I was not going to kill myself. I sat in the room with my towel and the pain swallowed me. Every part of me hurt. It needed to stop. I remembered learning in class that some people cut themselves to help anxiety. So, I took the blade to my leg and made my first cut. I felt as though I could exhale. "Nodia come now" my mom was ready to talk. She started off with "Nodia there is nothing you can say or do that will stop me from loving you, you know that". She kept on with the encouragement telling me that she loves me and that everything will be okay. I could've only thought to myself I'm so much more than this, I'm worth more than this. I was the president of a foundation for a group of kids who looked up to me. I'm an elected youth minister. People came to me for strength and this is what I had become? I was disgusted. Me and my mother began to argue, and I said to her "people don't get it, this is my reality. I don't have anything to offer a man. No virginity, no babies, no confidence. I have to wake up every day and accept that I am broken and accept that I am nothing." And the words my mother replied to me is what would change my life forever. She said "This is your reality. Your reality is that you are a beautiful, black young woman. You are a role model to young girls in your life. Your reality is that you have been burned and backstabbed and wronged, but your reality is that you have so much more to offer. Your reality is that you have helped so many through your exact situation. You can make your reality your past and it can fuel you. Stop hiding your scars, start showing them. Your scars show your strength. You are a survivor of trauma, rape, abuse, and of yourself. You are your hope, you are your future and you are your own champion. Look in the mirror and kiss your scars. Thank the lord above for leaving a mark of your triumph that you may never walk back down those roads, never fall for the same smiling faces and never ever doubt your worth EVER." It was those words that kept me for a time, but I was still angry, so angry. Until I met this girl.

The Girl with The Laugh

One day in high school sitting in class one girl caught my eye. I didn't know her, but she was laughing at a joke. It was her laugh that captivated me, it was genuine. I could feel her happiness across the classroom, it wasn't like the other kids, her happiness was different. She glowed, and quite honestly, I was jealous, so I mentioned her laugh, called it unruly and continued on my business. As class went on, ever so often I would catch myself staring at her, even with a straight face completing a writing assignment she looked graceful. The jealousy turned to hate. I began to concur stories about her in my mind thinking she must be a really mean person or justify her smile saying she probably had a privileged life that's why she was so happy. As five minutes took forever to go by my thoughts were interrupted by my friend who was trying to tell me something I can't even remember. Something pushed me out of my seat and I sat next to her. She looked at me as if she was expecting me to come. I didn't want to say it, she could not know about my story, it was mine. The tighter I clenched my jaw, the easier the words flew out of my mouth. "Do you think God will forgive someone who was raped and is not a virgin?" Looking back now I know that she was spiritually aware enough to unleash her evangelical spirit to save me. It was my moment and my time. She took her time encouraging me and for that moment everyone in the class disappeared I felt a warm tear roll down my cheek. UGH Weakness. I quickly wiped it away and looking around I saw all my peers staring at me wondering how much had happen to make someone like me cry in front of an entire classroom. She started praying for me, what in the name of Jesus was wrong with her, I was offended. A lot of situations gain control over us because we are too ashamed to claim it. Accepting her prayer would have meant I was as screw up as I thought I was. NO. Her prayer opened my chest cavity and made its way to my heart. I could feel the shift in the air I breathed at that very moment. I saw my brokenness in an image of a girl laying on the floor, crying, balled up in a fetal position, ripped clothing but something was happening to the ground it was changing from cement to tile, tile to dirt and from dirt to a field. It seemed no matter which floor my position was the same. I heard the words so clearly "It's time to change". Everything around me was changing and I was allowing my pain to keep me the same. Sarah Jakes-Roberts said at her woman evolve conference that "God didn't place you where you'd be comfortable, he placed you where you can grow." My burial ground had become a plantation for my birth. Seeds go through a particular process before growing where they must be dried up to a specific state before planting, they call it seed conditioning. My seed had been conditioned long enough and this young girl was planting me. "Paul plants, Apollos waters, but God gives the increase." It was my time, it was the appointed season. Suddenly everything I went through felt divinely purposed. I felt like Esther in the bible when her uncle said to her "who knows, maybe you were placed here for a such a time unto this". To present day I still have my Esther moments where I see the purpose in my condition stage. Can you see the purpose in your struggle? Is your past being reflected to you in someone else's life? Has someone been confiding in you? Have you been finding yourself in church regardless of circumstance? Could it be that you have been conditioned and place in that environment for "such a time like this?".

State of Mind

Your life experiences can reveal some truths about who you are as a person. It can reveal you to be loyal or deceitful. It can highlight strength or weakness. Things that we are comfortable speaking on but what about the underlying issues that linger in the backyard of our minds? How do we handle them? Anxiety, Depression, Personality Disorders, Suicidal Tendencies, Bipolar etc.? All these exist yet no one speaks on them. The world has created this stigma that mental illness deems someone incapable, so we hide. Do you know how many people are like you? It is quite common for people to experience anxiety and depression throughout life's stages. So why is it uncommon for people who live with these disorders to speak up? My experiences for that short amount of time had left me with bags that weighed down on my aspirations and dreams. It began to spill over into my work ethic and my daily life. An intense fear came over me all the time. I was always wondering who might try to hurt me. Wondering whether or not I'm safe. I was startled very easily, and most times over reacted to the slightest touch or noise. The situation was very difficult, but the experience taught me a lot about myself. Eventually things got worse, when I would get home late at my mother have to come outside and Get me, sometimes I would even stay home just to avoid having to go outside. It was really hard not knowing what kind of day it will be like before they even started. I was angry all the time. Everything irritated me, even my mother. And when things would get a really hard I would get pains in my chest and shortness of breath with this uncomfortable shaking in my hands. It was like I had no control over my body.

Anxiety

You know sometimes I get flashbacks… His hands, his breath, my pleas. Sometimes things happen that trigger me, and I still don't understand. Like loud talking in an enclosed space, I get really flustered. My head feels really light and my breathing shortens. I've noticed that opening the window helps, I have no idea why. I feel like the sound escapes and I can finally breathe. Sometimes when I see a man I get scared, so scared that I avoid many. If someone stared too deeply I would get uncomfortable to the point of irritability. Many times, people would comment on these behaviors as snotty and rude but baby they had no idea.

It seems to hit you at night doesn't it? When you've had a hard but productive day and you're feeling satisfied. You take a shower and you lay in bed thinking that you are about to get some sleep for tomorrow. NOPE. First you check your Instagram, someone just got married, someone else just bought a house. That friend who was sleeping on their mothers couch the other day? Well they finally got that business deal that they were working on. So, you get off the feed and decide to shift to the explore page, it's easier to look at people you don't know. You see a sixteen-year-old who got accepted to all ivy leagues schools and will be receiving a full scholarship for which ever one he chooses. You think to yourself, What the hell? I barely got accepted into my school. Suddenly its 2 am and you've already worked out that you will be poor the rest of your life, never find love and will never fulfill your dreams. And it all started with Instagram. I remember suddenly crying because of social media. So many people have anxiety because of it. This habit of comparing ourselves to others is so dangerous because we always come out weighing our self to be more or less valuable. Both are damaging to our growth because one allows you to become stagnant and takes away motivation to grow due to the idea that you are already on top and the other causes a wave of depression that diminishes self-worth and self-efficacy or causes you to overwork yourself trying to be like someone else. I remember wanting to have a body like those women on Instagram so bad. A thin waist, toned legs, a trimmed nose, full lips and straight hair. It was never that I thought I could not attain it (I mean plastic surgery duhh) but it was the fact that I thought I didn't measure up to other women without it. You know what's crazy is that I look pretty good, okay I'm being modest, I'm HOT. Like Cardi B would say, "you can tell from the front, I got it behind me". Maybe that was too far, deliver me Jesus! But yeah, **comparing myself to other people who had altered their appearance caused me to miss all the things I had going for myself.** It was exhausting. It was one of things I questioned often. Am I pretty? Will my boyfriend cheat on me with a prettier girl? God wasn't even in the picture anymore because there was a point in my life where I felt certain areas of my life relied on my appearance.

I would not even attempt to talk to a guy if my hair wasn't done and my outfit didn't meet the criteria of what I defined as sexy. I acknowledge my flaws before anyone would even notice and eventually I got into makeup. Makeup was therapeutic. My absolute favorite part was contouring, because I would give my nose this straighter appearance and I felt prettier because of it. I would add eye lashes and shape my brows to perfection. Eventually I couldn't leave the house without it and when I did I felt ugly. It took some looking back and seeing beauty in myself as a child without the makeup for me to have the courage to go without it. I still wear makeup but now it has a different value to me and now it is not the source of my beauty but simply compliments it.

Sitting in the chair of hairdresser today I am unaware of how I fell out of love with God. I feel so full of joy and peace that it's hard to picture a time when I didn't feel this way. Not that it's been so long it's just that the love has erased the pain. So now I see him with clear eyes.

On my first day of class while I sat at my desk my teacher walked in. He was a young Latino man standing at about 5'8 dressed in a suit. I was mesmerized y'all. Ain't nothing like a well-dressed man. While happily thinking about my good decision to take the class, I noticed that he had a scruffy beard and looked like his hair hadn't been cut. By the second class I realized he walked very funny, and during the third class I had made up mind that he was pretty rude. In the beginning I didn't catch the fine details because my vision was clouded by the suit and smooth tone. However, as time went on I began to see clearly. My environment for a long time clouded my vision, but **time revealed all truths.** And The truth in my life was that God is constant.

I fell out of love on my 20th Birthday, the first birthday that

I spent without my mother. I knew things weren't going to be the same since our parting, but I didn't expect no contact at all. I spent the entire morning crying. I buried myself under the covers and ignored all calls and texts except one. One of the prominent elders in my religion had called me. Not to say happy birthday but to just check on me. His name was King Shepherd Callendar. On the other end of the phone he said, "she didn't call you, didn't she?" I just remember hysterically crying to him on the phone and he listened, he told me to come see him at the church, so he can talk to me and we hung up. Going to see king shepherd was the most terrifying thing because he was an elder, was I really about to explain to him the life I was living? Could I really expose to him that "little Nodia" was not so little anymore? Impossible. It was decided I was going to his office and I was going to lie. When I came in he was with someone else, so I spent the time talking to a member of his congregation and hearing the testimony of a woman who told me the king shepherd had healed her. I'm guessing she thought that's what I was there for. When he came out I could see sadness in his eyes when he looked at me. We went to the office and he asked me how I was feeling I felt like immediately crying only a few people had asked me that since my life had turned into a soap opera. I told him the truth. Honestly at that time there was not much to tell I had one abusive encounter and was just partying at the moment. I told him I was not going back to church because I didn't want to make mommy uncomfortable. He said to me "I still see your innocence". I was confused I did not tell him I was abused. I only told him I was talking to guys. He said again "you still have your innocence". I was silent. As the tears fell down my face I listened to his counsel. "Nodia you still have your innocence, I see it." He was so sure. We talked for an hour about the events and as he promised me that my mother and I relationship would recover I told him that it wouldn't and never will. Mom told me the day my grandmother came that things will never be the same, but he was right. He was right about so much in my life. He saw me with clear eyes and during that time in my life and he became my symbol of hope. So, I stayed in church even though Jesus and I had beef, king shepherd had given me a light in my tunnel. Many meetings would follow as he nurtured the person I was behind the curtain. I loved him, and his passing showed me exactly how much. I honor him for the strong tower he has been in my life. As I still continue to grieve his presence in my life I will continue to honor his legacy by growing and Surpassing the dreams he had for me.

What had happened was…

You wanna know what helped me, my church. Being able to have men around me that I could trust and be alone with without feeling threatened or unsafe. Having women who told me I'm beautiful and blessed. My church was my haven. Life experiences had placed me the fetal position, but my church family nursed me back to life. They were my refuge. It was the only place I felt safe. When I decided it was time to show them my scars they validated me and told me it was okay. Teacher Rhonda who was always trying to make me comfortable shared her story and made me feel like I was not alone, Valerie who would talk to you to like an aunty though once you get her started she never stops lol, Corlette who epitomized strength and long suffering, Hillary who loved for real and never frowned EVER, Tony the man who I would marry if I was 60! The kids who only seen the good part of you. Jewel who was my sister and felt my pain. Chris who would always made me laugh and refused to let me shower alone after I had surgery (Literally stood behind the curtain). My twins Ann and Ann-Marie, Sophie my adult friend, Andrew the person who was the return of my giving in every single way, he saw me when others couldn't, he remembered me when others didn't, and he considered me, for that I am eternally grateful. See it wasn't literally Jesus who stepped into my life. It was my church who reintroduced me to him through their love and strength that led me on the journey of falling in Love again. I fell in love with the God in them and been in love ever since. See we can't see Christ, but we see him in others. I do not know where I would be if not for their display of Godliness.

They have stood by me through my life, burial and resurrection. Love the people around you who pour into who you are. Can you think of anyone? Someone who has gotten down and dirty with you and not only has supported but did the work too! Cherish them nurture them and when they mess up forgive them. They have fought hard for you allow those relationships to prosper along with your growth.

What it Look Like?
Imma' Baptist!

Spirit of faith, Come Down
Reveal the things of God
And make to us the Godhead Known,
And witness with the blood.

No man can truly say,
That Jesus is the Lord,
Unless he takes the Veil Away
And Breath the living Word.

That hymn has to be one of the mostly sung hymns in my faith. Wanna turn a Baptist church upside down? Just sing that. Just a heads up, we use faith synonymously with religion if you're wondering. They call us shouters. Mostly because we make really loud noises when we feel the Spirit of God. Sometimes I think that's all people see when they look at us, but we are so much more. We are Spiritual people, heavily relying on God for our future goals, awaiting plans and very next step. Growing up for me even with being the daughter of a pastor, church was just something I did on Sundays. Services were etched into my schedule without any invite. I never took interest or tried to understand the origin of my faith. The speaking in tongues, the throwing of water (and I do mean THROWING of water), the earthen and brass vessels the all held a different significance, and our long dresses made up of such vibrant colors, headwraps according to spiritual height and even jewelry that symbolized our spiritual journeys. It all seemed like too much until I fell in love with Christ and felt him for myself.

God Plays Dress Up

It's important that everyone realizes that difference doesn't have to mean separation, just because someone practices their beliefs in a different way it doesn't mean that their relationship with our savior will hold a different outcome. There's a reason why your stomach turns when you see a practitioner of another Faith, and there is meaning behind why Jehovah Witnesses get on your nerves and let me not get you started on the Jewish Faith. You don't like them ideally because they are different and that's okay baby! God takes on different meanings for each believer. Can I go to church right quick? God will meet you on your level sugar! If your level is weeping tears of joy when he shows up then so be it, and if someone else's level may be running up and down the aisles like the building is on fire don't judge. Everyday people both associated with and outside of my religion (which is Spiritual Baptist) judge us because we are different. I am aware that the diverse religious/spiritual populations across the world are influenced by different doctrines. However, the vital necessity of Christian practical living trumps the affirmation and validation of any religious creed. It is essential that everyone's life echo's obedience as Abraham, Repentance as David, and Conviction as Paul. During the inception of my knowledge I regarded my spiritual journey as my own but as I evolved it was clear that my call was not inclusive to only me, it was more than me. Through deeper meditation and analysis of the scripture, I believe that the Kingdom walk can be looked at from a holistic point of view and that it must house purpose. All I really said there is Let your LIFE be a Testament of your belief.

"It's not about you" as one of my ex boyfriends would repeatedly tell me. It's a beautiful thing when you've evolved from "when is my time" to "How can I make the time I have productive by helping someone else". A lot of times our endeavors are not fruitful because they are not purposeful. Running around doing things for no reason of course you'll stop when you get tired, you have no reason to keep going. What's driving you? What's motivating you? Is it Family? Friends? God? There must be something encouraging your growth or stunting it. As my mother once said in a sermon she gave "whether in church or out of church, you want to know what's in it for you!". Work without purpose is difficult and tiring. Purpose causes a sense of confidence to come over someone. My driving force lies behind all the wonderful things that God has blessed me with. I find myself constantly trying to be aware of what's driving me whether the feeling be positive or negative, that way I know how to maintain the positive and discard the negative. **The presence of self-awareness is the acquisition of real power.** To control one's self is to be in control of one's environment and the once you can control your surroundings you are now in the place to press towards your purpose. Self is the beginning of the kingdom journey and the complete understanding of self is knowing that you are a small part of a worldwide picture. When you look at yourself through a holistic perspective you'll better understand the specific part that you have been designed to play. So, don't be caught up in your unfortunate situation, look forward. The time in your life when You're coming out of a toxic situation is so beautiful. You are at your best, you're passionate, motivated. Bask in your imperfection. Some of my best sermons, best moments, highest level of worship, powerful friendships were while I was a walking disaster. That world-wind has spun me into the beautiful being that I am becoming. Don't stress, your breakthrough is inevitable, so in the meantime work, grind, pray, read and help people. Most importantly never forget where you were when your silver lining comes, let that dark past keep you living in light.

The Baptist Experience

The Church is my base. You know when you meet someone and the sign for when things are getting serious is meeting the family? Well you can meet my family any time but baby if I bring you to church ISSA RELATIONSHIP for real. Although I am in a constant state of worship through my life living, allowing you to see me in church worshipping, shouting, crying etc. is exposing myself to someone in a very vulnerable way. Not only because I consider it a very intimate part of my life but because a lot of times my church can be misunderstood. Just imagine someone who has no experience with African culture seeing people dancing, throwing water (and I do mean THROWING water), speaking in tongues, ringing bells all at the same time? To many, this is a beautiful and enriching experience, but to some it is overwhelming, and this created a sense of shame in me as a young girl.

I first realized I was ashamed of my religion when I was

eleven years old. All the kids at my church were given the simple task of inviting a friend. The moment we were asked to do it was when I knew I never wanted anyone to know that I am a spiritual Baptist. Not because I didn't like my religion but because I didn't understand it. I had no idea why I did the things I did because I had made no attempt to understand. I couldn't value what I didn't understand. As I got older I was less secretive because my dress code was accepted and really in my generation of spiritual Baptist there are much more young people than the generation prior, so I had company. I didn't have to go to the store after church by myself. I ran into people in my religion everywhere and it made me less self-conscious but not less embarrassed. I became truly proud of my religious culture and Christian belief (notice how they are two separate things, but that's for another book lol) when I began to listen in church. In my religion, along with the word, along with the worship, along with the water throwing, testimonies and manifestations of the holy spirit there are lectures and lessons. The elder might stop in the middle of everything to tell a story or parable, he may take time to unfold and reveal some of the mysteries of the religion and the way we worship but you will never understand if you don't listen. A long time ago my mother who is also my spiritual leader and pastor told me "Never let anyone make you think that you are not enough because you don't know the mysticism of our faith, if you know God, you know enough". My spiritual father once told me the secrets of our faith is in our bible. I've come to realize that the more I read. The more I read, the more I understand myself, my journey and Christ and the more those three things integrate the more I am enlightened about my spirituality. So, as I listened to the elders in my church the more gems I identified in my religion. Now you may not identify with my religion but that's okay, you can still apply it to yourself. What part of yourself or your spirituality are you ashamed of? Are you intimidated to say you are saving yourself because of religious values? Have you ever omitted the fact that you are a Christian when describing who you are? Along with studying yourself, explore your spirituality and find where they meet. It will allow you to become a whole person.

Being a Spiritual Baptist is one of the hardest things there is. There is way more work entailed than with other religions. I remember telling someone I was cleaning my church and they said, "don't you have a janitor?". I thought to myself "what kind of church does he go to?". There is literally a surplus of physical labor along with the normal duties of any church member. This is why one of the greatest characteristics about being Baptist is the fact that you have family. We cook together, eat together, read together and build bonds that cannot be broken. I believe the thing that forms many friendships is how much we labor TOGETHER. Being around one another so often helps create a greater sense of unity. In our church we practice the Rites of Fasting, otherwise known as mourning or pointing. Not to get into something I have no clue how to begin to explain, but it is one of our most sacred practices. It is where a person denies themselves of all worldly things and set themselves apart to spend time with God. It is not only the absence of food, but also one would abstain from technology, social interactions etc. Anything that would be seen as a distraction would be removed for a certain period of time. This is one of rituals accountable for the spiritual Baptist church's family like structure. We eat together, sleep together, worship together, cry together and laugh together. However, I must admit this same tight knot bond is the reason for our demise. When you are that close to people you see their faults and it makes for a more turbulent relationship. Still I have not seen a place filled with more love.

Rent your Heart

"And rend your heart, and not your garments, and turn unto the LORD your God: for he is gracious and merciful, slow to anger, and of great kindness, and repenteth him of the evil."

Joel 2:13

I think my favorite part about church is the clothes. You can literally walk into a Spiritual Baptist Church and the outfits alone can help you identify what stage that believer is at in their Kingdom Journey. As time went on though, those ideologies were relaxed and Thank God for it because clothes were only given according to the principles of our religion and not according to those of Christlike living; granting us masqueraders who paraded themselves as Leaders. Being young and witnessing the anointing of masqueraders made me feel righteous. I had never felt more holy and morally competent in my life than when I allowed myself to witness the downfall of the forerunners of my faith. Right about now, you'd probably want to hear about the hypocrisy of leaders and all the things that make them not worthy, but my conviction doesn't allow me to convict others. If you're finding yourself thinking of that one Bishop/Leader/Mother that doesn't deserve their seat, Check your motives babe. Their ability to lead is not for us to determine. It's important that we remember that **the chosen will always be chosen** and that we are not the Savior, Jesus is. Failure to see things from this perspective creates a bitter member. Those are what I like to call Sour patch members. You know those members that's only coming because of ONE pastor, or the ones that's just here for the word they don't want to get caught up with THEM folks, the members that come late and leave early to avoid socializing. Made sour by their circumstances but sweet through the love of God. Sometimes they're up, sometimes they're down kind of folks. I know why it upsets you, the problem is that you are NOT sometime-ish, you have Jesus ALL the time, so you're annoyed at the member who only shakes your hand when praise and worship was good, or who only speaks to you when the preaching touched them. As someone who has been both accused and the accuser, I can say that attitudes like this are only broken by Prayer and Soul searching. The Sour patch member has no idea how quick their mood changes, its one moment that has led them to be this way most of their lives. SOUR, SWEET and if given the wrong response from you, eventually GONE. Always remember your power to change the situation, **you're salt, act like it**.

I think that Joel wanted to send a message that the formalities should stop. It was time to get our hands dirty even if it meant the ripping apart of our very own heart. Intense right? Have you ever considered that it's your own heart that needs to be shredded? It's so hard when the word that will resurrect you has to kill you first. Pushing past brokenness and pain to pursue something that resembles a new beginning but seems too good to be true. Circling your redemption and promise of a better life to afraid to enter into the unknown. You can do it. You can start over. You can get that divorce. You can heal from the pain. You can. A pronoun and a verb have never been more powerful together. You can, you are able, you are permitted to be happy, to be better, to be whole. It is not too much, and you are not too far. Do me a favor, trust God. When you begin to drown don't stretch your arms out and struggle to find him. Let go, Surrender. Allow him to reach down, stretch down and pull you up. As the old Baptist would say "out of the miry clay and unto solid ground". So, what you're broken. And what? A broken and contrite heart cannot be bypassed by a God who specializes in HEART MATTERS.

6

The Heart of the Matter

Her heart is remolding. Piece by piece. She understands now.
Her Call. Her Gift. Her Voice.
It's different.
Her voice carries pain inflicted with no reason.
Her anointing walks before her. She is Favored and Is blessed at the cost of a shattered heart and deflated pride.
But… Her heart is restored through HIM.
HE is the healer, the comforter, the mender of brokenness and the lover of her soul.
He is what matters and he deals with the matters of her heart.

Can I pinpoint the exact moment I fell in love with Jesus for the second time? Nah I can't. See the love snuck up on me over time. One minute I was being reintroduced and the next I was head over heels for him. I remember sitting in church thinking "this is it for me". It had gotten as good as it ever could, and I would have to accept that. I was okay with mediocrity, but those people, those Baptist people. They refused to let me be lost. Constantly people would have dreams and visions warning to change my life, other elders in churches would encourage me to stay strong and do the right thing and I would hear but never listen. They kept loving me. I believe they set the foundation for change and then allowed it to happen I was never forced.

Take a minute and visualize your place of worship. Think about the structure and the color of the walls, the comfy-ness of the chairs, is your choir really that good? Now visualize the members and think about the member who has a lot going on, the man who is only here for the women, the kids who are only showing up because their parents forced them, and of course our favorite member that makes you ask yourself, is she faking the spirit AGAIN? BLOCK OUT THOSE CONCERNS! The place where you worship was made to accommodate your body not your spirit. We don't belong here, and we SHOULD be uncomfortable sometimes. Is it too comfy? Maybe You might be too complacent. That member that has a lot going on, how can you help? A prayer, resource, sewing a seed into their lives can make a difference. Many times, we hold on to formalities and ideologies of what the appropriate and Blessed church looks like and we hold our sisters and brothers to these ineffective and fruitless standards. We're too busy working on someone else and not ourselves. Let me explain. The answer is to teach the value and not the skill. The moment you focus on skill a shift of perspective takes place where it's more important to successfully preach the scripture without living it and Christian living becomes a burden instead of blessing, because serving God to you is only objective. For example: I never stole because I was always too scared of my mother finding out. Because I had no value system behind my actions, I did eventually steal one day. Teaching values takes away the stronghold that God refused to put on us in the first place. he believed that we should have a choice; and that choice allows us to make righteousness a part of our identity rather than the outcome of a formality. We no longer display righteousness, but we become it. What does holiness look like? It looks like you! Too often we make perfection seem unattainable and that often becomes the justification behind why we fail to thrive. Perfection is maturation. I'm not exactly a bible scholar but I do not remember perfection in the bible being described as elusive. In fact, it seemed very accessible to me through process. And to what is the process? I have no answer. I cannot determine anyone's process because we are all different and we each have our own call. I cannot define my process because to each test there will be another that follows. Its less about defining the process and more about chartering it. The process is defined as you navigate it. The more you press forward, the more your history/story is created.

People spend an enormous amount of time trying to save others when Christ invites us to first embark on a journey of becoming saved before saving. There must be some aspect of completeness on your life before you go trying to complete someone else. Yes, he wants us to help people, but can you do that if you are not helping yourself? Christ shifts the perspective and encourages us to undress ourselves in the presence of unblemished mirrors and trusted masters who can help us identify our areas of barrenness. The unblemished mirror is the word of God. Whenever you hear the word you see yourself and the only mirror that is true unblemished is his word. Most times we enjoy our blemished and funhouse mirrors that gives us an image that we would prefer, but in the long run they not only damage our sight but also our future. The good thing about this is that there are masters. Masters are people who have matured in the craft of living a Christ like life. What I'm hinting to is that you need a home, a base. Somewhere that you can see your reflection clearly without bias. Now I know you may be thinking, "the church is not as real as you think", though I cannot vouch for every church I can tell you that it's important not to generalize an entire people based on some experiences. Your church sucks find a new one.

Your church is an investment in yourself you are looking for a place where you can be nurtured so spend real time looking for somewhere that fits your belief and your personality. Take time and try to meet the pastor. Sometimes the members reflect a behavior that is the total opposite of the pastor's beliefs and though it may be offsetting it happens. Grow duck skin and let it roll of your back. If you truly understand how much you need healing and how much you need Christ, then it will be easier to persevere and endure through issues and minor setbacks.

Your fruitfulness is dependent on your ability to recognize your need for self-improvement. Nurture yourself. While most people may think its sitting at home with your bible and preaching to yourself, its actually finding a home and taking time to build positive and therapeutic bonds with people who are like minded. I once told my church hat everything they are looking for is in the church. What better friend you can have than one at church who understands your mindset and is aware that your life is intertwined with your call. Now those are people to have in your circle. Plus, speaking from a church going person point of view, when you slip and slide you want people that are going to encourage you to be better not someone who is going to sarcastically say "I thought you was a Christian?".

You want to grow in all parts of your life not some. You don't want distorted growth. Distorted comes from the Latin root words Dis=apart and Torquere=to twist which can be translated to "to twist to one side" or "to twist apart". Why are you only succeeding in one aspect of your life which for most believers is church and fail to see the manifestation of God in everyday life? It's because we only know and see ourselves from a limited point of view. We only nurture the parts that feel good. Our past experiences, pre-conceived notions and even our failure to make the right choices causes us to twist to one side. For me it was all the those things. What is it for you? Take a look at your life, it can be evidence of the cracks in your character or proof of your kingdom building lifestyle. Don't mistake my tone and think that everyone fights this battle. Some of us are trying hard and doing the right thing. To those who have learned balance and maintenance, my words to you are its time to take a risk. Don't be boring! Do something new. There is another level waiting for you, another ceiling to be broken, a new adventure to explore. Don't settle, because even positive stagnancy can be toxic. We don't want toxic, we want organic. All our negative experiences can be broken. Generational curses, depression, suicidal thought, trauma can be overcame. **Pain must be acknowledged to be addressed.** Maybe you're in the same place because you haven't broken your strongholds. So what! There is still time. You must transition like a plant that has become too big for its environment, exit your carnal mindset of limits and enter the realm of spiritual wholeness and maturity with Christ that empowers you to do all things. Evolve and escape the shackles of the world that trains you to live in hypocrisy and pretend that your whole when the world and everything that he did was to heal our brokenness. I don't have to hear your story to know that you are broken or Have been broken I just have to know that Jesus lived.

THE BIRTH OF HER

"Forever here my rest shall be,
Close to thy bleeding side
Tis all my hope and all my plea
For me the savior died"
She sits and looks at the corpse of the girl she once knew. Unaware of how she got to this point but thankful. The sacrifice that was made for her to live is great. So, she acknowledges the girl that once lived unapologetically because, that girl gave way to the woman that birthed.
New me, Who Dis?

I sat in a viewing service tied up in my own emotions. I looked around and there was sadness everywhere. It took me straight back to the only death that ever affected me, King Shepherd. (I told you I would get to it) People were pretending, putting on good faces trying to stay strong, others weeping bitterly, many there just for support. Then there was me, I had no real ties with anyone there. I was simply there because my parents were. I was having an extremely rough time and my mother did not want to leave me home, so I packed my bags and signed up to watch folks cry. As I sat I watched and wondered what role I would play if I had an immediate family member like my mom pass away. Would I be strong and hold it all together pushing my pain away, would I be a mess so much that I could not function, would I become bitter towards the people who were never there for her? I sat as I imagined what it would like if I were in that position. I was interrupted when I was being introduced to a ninety-one-year-old woman. Death is so funny isn't it? There I was at a home-going for a young vibrant woman and in the front row sat a woman who had lived for over nine decades.

It so confusing sometimes to see bad things happening to you. Especially when everyone around you seems to be getting along just fine. Now that I'm the person getting along just fine, I find myself spotting those in need much quicker. It was my experience, it takes one to know one I guess. I would be pulled toward these broken individuals and the walking dead. Sometimes they'd find it strange that I even noticed them. They have no idea that I saw a reflection of the old me in their eyes. SO, there I was with a life that was happier than most, a bank account that was close to empty but a heart that was ready to give. I need to do more I thought. I sat in the car on my way to the mall and said out loud, "God if you do it for me, I'll have more people lovin' on you than you'd ever imagine".

Ms. Attitude

I was at work one day and I needed some help, so I called the manager and ask them to send someone over. Moments later a woman showed up at the front door. As I opened the door I said "hi, how are you?" she proceeded to walk inside. I did what I normally and blocked the door. "I'm sorry I don't know everyone's faces, you are?". Obviously annoyed the woman said "didn't you call for help? You want me to show you my ID?". You know ya girl said "Yes". She showed me her ID and I let her in.

This lady was so upset because she thought I should've known who she was. I'd like to think that's how the creator looks at us sometimes. Could you imagine showing up at his door tryna walk up on him? Like who are you? I know when I meet him I'm tryna have some credentials. Its why I do everything I do. It's for GOD. I've never felt more powerful than when I was doing his work, I've never felt more vulnerable than when I was in his presence, I've never felt more hopeful than when I witnessed his goodness. He is my End Game. It is that determination that has birthed the woman writing to you now.

When you look at me, what do you see?
Do you see a woman forgotten or a girl remembered?
She is a phoenix.
Her strength is in her bones and her vulnerability in her flesh.
Not knowing has always been her solace,
Because the one on whom she depends knows all things.
Grace is in her back pocket, confidence in her sway
She is the type of woman only a bad bod can handle but only a
man of God can get
None can define her
Because every day she creates a new meaning of what it means to be
Black, a Woman, and Spiritual Baptist.

The way I see it, a situation will either motivate or intimidate you. Which one are you choosing? The love does not exempt you from pain. The second time can mean a second heartbreak or another letdown. It is the assurance of always having someone that keeps us going. I think I'll share something with you because I believe it will enlighten and empower you. Trust me, I am not too excited about sharing my business yall.

Because of the messy timeline I've given you I think I should share with you that I have been celibate for a little over two years I think. Now much to your surprise the strength of this journey came from the fact that I was not over my last relationship. Don't get me wrong I met guys. Great guys. However, there was always this lingering feeling of I will get back with my ex and we'll live happily ever after, blah blah blah. So, there I was minding my business when I was invited to an event that he would also be attending. UGH. Anxiety took over me yall. After a couple pep talks from my mother and my nieces I felt better and soon after it would be the day of the event. I stepped in and scanned the crowd for him, found him. OMG run. I didn't. I kept my head straight and minded my business. I looked again, and we were wearing the same print "we were meant to be" I thought. Lol (it's funny now but trust me yall it wasn't then) Throughout the night I had my highs and lows, but I was doing pretty okay until someone said to me, "is that his girlfriend?". RUN Nodia. I looked at the captain of my support team I brought with me that night with tears in my eyes. But the night wasn't about me it was about a beautiful soul I had the privilege to know so I redirected my thoughts. I decided that I should enjoy the night and spent the time appreciating my friends who were around me. That beautiful night ended and retreated home to my bed to cry, just a little. The next day I sulked and ate junk food and took care of myself after the loss I took the previous night. I'm okay now. So, let me make my point.

Your second time will not always be a bed of roses. Sometimes the second time will be painful, and God will bring you back to a situation to shut the door in your face. I won't lie, it hurts. The beautiful thing about the end of a season is that whether or not it was good is no longer relevant, because its over. Your situation may have been horrible, but you've been harboring and allowing it to control you. This time around God says no more! He brings you back to that painful place and he puts a stop to it and says, "NOT MY BABY". He swoops in and put a "The End" on that painful chapter and suddenly your smiling because you have a new page. Write my love and do it unapologetically.

(Whew, I was wondering where that was going, lol)

Unfortunately, this is our end my dear. I do not wish to add anything that was not placed in my heart, so I leave you with this…

My loves I am still growing every day and I have not reached my peak, and that's okay. I want you to know that if you are not where you want to be that it's okay. I still gotta borrow twenty dollars from my mom, I still want her to take me to the doctor, I still refer to myself as a girl forgetting how grown I actually am, I still make bad choices.

That's the thing about giving birth to someone new, you have no idea which way it'll go. I guess you're just gonna have to wait for the next book huh?

Acknowledgements

Jehovah

Who am I? That you have decided to think of me? Every day with you is sweeter than the day before. The more I discover your infinite love for me, the more I intentionally love others. At this moment I still question your wisdom in relation to this book. What do I say when I am told it's too short? Or it has no specific Genre? However, I have never felt more secure in my call. I remember asking you what my gift is, some days I'm still not sure if I know, but **I do know** that you are real. And to me, that's all that ever had and ever will matter!

Mom

I don't know if any of this would be possible without your relentless will to empower me and mold me into the woman I am becoming today. I believe that it is the example that you have set for me which has allowed me to experience love in its purest form. The regard that I hold you in sometimes challenges the first commandment but because your transparency has allowed me to view the source of your strength, I too have chosen to abide in him who is omnipotent.

Grandma

I could imagine your attitude when you saw your swift appearance in this book, but I must say that your presence in this God inspired memoir has no

resemblance to your presence in my life. Thank
you for putting my welfare first always.

Toy-Toy

I think that your love has always been an oasis in my
life. Though you cannot identify your place in my life,
I see it clearly. Your spirit is revealed in this book in so
many hidden ways and it bears witness to the pillar that
you have been in my life. Cheers to our SOUL-Ship!

King Shepherd

To this day when someone compliments my craft or speaks
highly of my character I touch the earth in remembrance
of you and the humility that you displayed. You once said
that "Touching the earth, reminds us where we came
from, the earth.". It has been my own personal way of
acknowledging your presence in my life. Thanking you
for seeing me full grown and for watering my potential.

My Readers (Heyyyy Babiesss)

Can you feel it? I am sending my love and my strength to
you at this moment. Thank you for taking time to read
this God-inspired work in a time where everything is in a
video. You've allowed this fearful woman to bare herself
in efforts to send a message, and that is that "you can fall
in love again". This journey with you was amazing. I have
cried, doubted and screamed my frustrations onto these

pages and I am hoping that you heard me. I know that some people won't believe or understand, I am aware that many of my perspectives will enrage you or conflict with your beliefs. The goal was not to have you agree but to have you engage and whether it be positive or negative I am just thankful for your whatever feeling you experience as a result of this work. The beauty of this work is that there is always another chance. So maybe you are about to fall in love for a 3rd or 4th time, who cares! At least there is opportunity and room at the alter for you to try again. I love you, for real. I pray your strength, peace and prosperity in all your endeavors. Until next time, Sugar.

Picture of HEDM

House of Esther Divine Ministries

580 empire Blvd. Brooklyn NY 11225

YouTube: House of Esther Divine Ministries

IG@ nodiasamuels

Facebook- Sherene Samuels

CPSIA information can be obtained
at www.ICGtesting.com
Printed in the USA
FFHW022343210319
51103617-56535FF